Y0-DKB-012

Practical Answers to Common Questions About Sex in Marriage

Practical Answers to Common Questions About Sex in Marriage

Tim and Beverly LaHaye

PYRANEE
BOOKS

Zondervan Publishing House
Grand Rapids, Michigan

PRACTICAL ANSWERS TO COMMON QUESTIONS
  ABOUT SEX IN MARRIAGE
Copyright © 1984 by The Zondervan Corporation

Pyranee Books are published by Zondervan
Publishing House, 1415 Lake Drive, S.E.,
Grand Rapids, Michigan 49506

Library of Congress Cataloging in Publication Data

LaHaye, Tim F.
  Practical answers to common questions about sex in marriage.

  1. Sex—Religious aspects—Christianity—Miscellanea.
2. Sex in marriage—Miscellanea. I. LaHaye, Beverly. II. Title
HQ31.L232   1984   306.7'3   84-7373
ISBN 0-310-27042-1

Printed in the United States of America

84 85 86 87 88 89 90 / 10 9 8 7 6 5 4 3 2

*To all those who believe married love
can be beautiful, exciting, and fulfilling
and to those who wish
they could believe*

Tim and Beverly LaHaye

Answer Your Questions on Sex in Marriage

Sex is such a major part of life, and because it is so private, most people endure many unanswered questions on it all through their lives. They range from morality to skill, positions, frequency, size, and many others. The field is limitless! And almost everyone has some questions.

During the past 13 years, my wife and I have held over 450 family seminars for audiences totaling more than half a million people. At most of these seminars we asked the participants to submit questions concerning family living. More than 50 percent of these questions pertained to sexual adjustment. A sex questionnaire which we administered to more than 3,400 people before writing our book, *The Act of Marriage*, contained a space at the end for important sex questions. Almost every survey response included one or more questions. The obvious need for help on this score greatly influenced us to write *The Act of Marriage*, in which we included many of the answers to the most commonly asked questions. This booklet contains "the cream" of those questions with their answers plus a few new ones.

Many of our answers will be different from those given by the popular sex writers of our day. We make no apology for this, because we are committed to the authority of the Bible, testing all problems and ideas by its principles. We believe that the key to happiness is to know the principles of God and do them (John 7:17). Secular writers are usually humanists who start with the fallacious premise that man is an animal and can satisfy his basic drives and passions in any way he desires as long as he doesn't hurt someone else. By contrast, we believe that man is a special creation of God and that the Bible is His manual on human behavior. Where the Bible speaks clearly on a subject, therefore, we will probably be 180° in opposition to the humanistic viewpoint.

Two reasons convince us that obedience to biblical principles on this delicate subject produces far greater happiness than does the philosophy of humanism:

1. Biblical principles come from a loving, all-knowing God who understands what is best for man (His special creation).
2. We have seen so many miserable devotees of humanism switch to biblical principles and find happiness that we are convinced they work.

One thing should be kept in mind when a person answers life's questions from the Bible: God's Word doesn't cover every single facet of married love in detail. Thus it is easy to be swayed by traditions or opinions that may not be grounded in Scripture, but instead are carry-overs from past cultural practices or standards. We have tried to be fair in such matters and strip ourselves of unscriptural prejudices when answering these questions. Where the Bible speaks clearly we speak positively; where the Bible is silent, we offer our opinion.

ABORTION
Is it ever right for a Christian to have an abortion?

A crucial issue in today's society relates to the morality of abortion. Ever since the 1973 Supreme Court ruling granted a constitutional guarantee of privacy in such matters and left the decision to the individual woman during the first six months of her pregnancy, legalized abortions have increased at a catastrophic rate. Many opponents of abortion warned that if it were made legal, it would result in promiscuity, infidelity, venereal disease, and guilt. Who can deny the accuracy of their forecast?

There are two kinds of abortions—natural and induced. Although medical science cannot always tell why, some women abort their pregnancies naturally, which may be nature's way of dealing with birth defects or other prenatal complications. Induced abortions are medically simple if performed by a competent doctor in the early stages of pregnancy. There are two reasons for inducing an abortion: (1) when such action is necessary to save the life of the mother—called a "therapeutic abortion"; and (2) for the convenience of the mother, because she is either unmarried or does not want the child. In such cases those making such a decision must bear the moral responsibility for their actions.

Dr. C. Everett Koop, U.S. Surgeon General, says that a choice between saving the life of the mother or the life of the child is so extremely rare that it is just a smoke screen used by abortionists to advance their permissive practice. Even when necessary, such a decision usually is made at the *end* of pregnancy, not at the beginning, when most abortions occur. In the majority of cases, the mother's life can be spared by taking the child

6

through a Caesarean section the seventh or eighth month, when both child and mother have an excellent chance to survive.

In recent years we have come to realize that even in rape cases there is no justification for abortion. All counselors, of course, should advise a "D and C" or other cleansing treatment by approved medical doctors immediately after such a traumatic experience *before* conception occurs. Such a procedure is therapeutically safe, and since life has not been "propagated" yet (or conceived, if you prefer), it is not murder.

To see the high regard for human life reflected in the Bible, read Exodus 21:22–23, which taught the children of Israel that the unborn child deserves the same protection as any other living human. It instructs that if a pregnant woman loses her child prematurely because a man happens to injure her, the man should be put to death. Obviously the Bible regards the unborn fetus as a truly living human being. We can do no less.

Abortion on demand has reached frightening proportions today. One report indicates that since the 1973 Supreme Court legalized such murders, more than 15,000,000 abortions have been performed in the U.S. Christians need to understand that the Bible, not the Supreme Court, is our basis for morality. We should all work for the defeat of any political leader who votes for abortion. He obviously does not have a sufficiently high regard for human life to represent the Christian community on this or other moral issues.

We hear a great deal today from the feminist movement about "a woman has a right to choose— it's her body." And it is right! A woman does have the right to choose, *before* she gets pregnant. After that there is another life that must be considered.

Whether it is one minute or nine months after conception, the mother's "choice" is life or death to another living soul. If she chooses "death," that is murder. How any Christian can maintain silence while over 4,000 murders called "abortion" are committed *daily* is beyond us. And as long as our tax money is used to fund some of them, we should all use our influence both at the polls and by letters to our legislators to halt this holocaust.

When I was a teenager I had an abortion. Years later I became a Christian. Now I have a family, but I am still troubled by what I have done. Will I ever get over this feeling of guilt?

Pro-abortionists rarely discuss the enormous guilt that often follows an abortion. I well recall conducting a funeral for a twenty-one-year-old woman who had committed suicide after hers!

Thankfully, the Bible guarantees that the blood of Jesus Christ cleanses us of *all sin,* including abortion (1 John 1:7–9). I suggest two procedures that will help you to deal with your guilt: (1) Do a Bible study on *God's forgiveness;* (2) After having asked God's forgiveness for that specific sin, thank Him by faith for His forgiveness each time you recall the experience. Gradually your feelings of guilt will fade from view.

One of the tragic realities of life is that, even though we experience God's forgiveness, it is often difficult to forgive ourselves. We suffer the consequences of sins and mistakes, and the physical and emotional problems that frequently result from an abortion are grim reminders of this fact. Yet we can become better, stronger persons for having endured tragedy, sorrow, and forgiveness.

ADULTERY
Can a person truly be forgiven of adultery?

The sins of adultery, homosexuality, and murder were held as capital crimes in the Bible, as evidenced by the death penalty (Lev. 20:10). Clearly, human life is of prime importance in the Word of God, and these sins affect the perpetuity of life. In spite of that, Jesus Christ's sacrifice on the cross is sufficient to cleanse these or any other sins (1 John 1:7, 9). Further evidence of God's pardon of this sin appears in Jesus' forgiveness of the woman taken in adultery (John 8:1–11) and the woman with five husbands who was living with still another (John 4:1–42).

Can a Christian commit adultery?

A Christian is potentially capable of committing any sin known to man, but if he is "born again," he cannot avoid the ensuing guilt of the Holy Spirit (John 16:7–11). For that reason Paul challenges Christians to walk in the motivation of the Spirit, not in the motivation of the flesh (Gal. 5:16–21). If a Christian harbors evil thoughts in his mind over a period of time, he will ultimately perform their actions. That is why Christ equated evil, lustful thoughts with adultery (Matt. 5:28). In this day of abundant sexual temptation it is imperative to guard one's thought life.

How can I forgive myself for being unfaithful to my partner?

Infidelity is among the most devastating blows to a marriage, creating a series of harmful results, not the least of which is the guilt that engulfs the

9

transgressor. We have seen such a guilt drive the offender to a nervous breakdown. The Scripture says, "The way of transgressors is hard" (Prov. 13:15); that is particularly true of sexual sins.

All self-forgiveness begins with God's forgiveness. Once the realization grips you that your confession of that sin in the name of Jesus Christ has cleansed you from *all* unrighteousness, you will begin to forgive yourself. Two things can hasten this: (1) Get a Bible concordance and write down every verse in Scripture on the subject of forgiveness of sin, then read them over several times; (2) On the basis of 1 John 1:9, every time you remember your sin, pause long enough to thank God by faith that He has forgiven you. Gradually you will learn to accept forgiveness as a fact rather than condemn yourself for confessed sin.

How can I forgive my partner for his unfaithfulness?

There is probably no greater betrayal of trust than marital infidelity; consequently it is not uncommon for the offended partner to find great difficulty in forgiving his or her mate. But anguish and resentment must not be perpetuated, for though it is understandable, resentment is no basis upon which to build a relationship. That is why many couples break up after an adulterous escapade, even when it is concluded with repentance and the offender discontinues such conduct.

Our Lord taught the necessity of forgiveness in Matthew 6:14–15; Ephesians 4:32; and many other passages. God never commands us to do what He will not enable us to do; therefore, if you *want* to forgive, you can. But if you wish to harbor bitterness and bear a grudge, you will probably never get over it. I challenged one offended wife with that problem. "Do you want to be happy the rest of your life or miserable? It's up to you!"

I have confessed my sin of adultery to God and have no intention of repeating it. Should I tell my partner?

Although other factors must be considered that are not included in this brief question, we ordinarily do not recommend telling the offended partner in such cases when the following conditions are met:

1. Genuine repentance and confession of the sin to God;
2. Severing the illicit relationship and avoiding any contact with the other party;
3. The establishment of spiritual safeguards, i.e., a daily prayer and quiet time, regular church participation, and an honest talk with one's minister.

Once adultery has been committed, can you ever trust your partner again? Doesn't one offense make others easier?

This all depends on whether he has repented of his sin, confessed it to God and to you, and has broken off all contact with the other person. If these have occurred, you would be wise to give your mate every chance to prove his sincerity by forgiving and forgetting the past. If not, you will only teach him that he can "have his cake and eat it too."

This should be a time for you to evaluate your life honestly to search for ways you might change your own attitudes and behavior so that, with God's help in applying biblical principles, you might become the best possible partner spiritually, emotionally, and physically. When a husband or wife is unfaithful, there is usually some definite lack in the faithful mate in meeting the other's desires and needs.

In any marriage in which one or both partners is a Christian, the couple should exhaust all resources before deciding to obtain a divorce, even when one is an adulterer. Divorce should always be the last resort after many sincere attempts at reconciliation.

BIRTH CONTROL

Is it right for Christians to practice birth control?

Every couple practices some form of birth control, for otherwise families would be much larger than they are. If the partners do not use one or more of the various scientific methods, they at least practice abstinence during the wife's most fertile time. However, this seems unfair to the wife, because that is the time when she would find lovemaking most enjoyable. Rather than cheat her out of the pleasure God designed for her to enjoy in marriage, it would be better to use a proven contraceptive. We believe God does not oppose limiting the size of one's family to the number of children one can effectively raise to serve Him; we do think He never intended parents to use birth control devices to exclude children. They are "an heritage of the Lord" (Ps. 127:3) and a great source of blessing that every couple should desire.

Doesn't God's displeasure with Onan in his spilling his seed on the ground indicate that He opposes birth control?

If that kind of reasoning were used in the slaying of Ananias and Sapphira in Acts 5, one could conclude that God opposes a person's selling his possessions and giving the return as an offering to Him. In both instances, however, God slew the people because they pretended to do one thing, but did another. In Genesis 38:8–10 we read that Onan cheated his brother out of his rightful heritage by refusing to father a child in his brother's name, as was the custom in his day. Thus it is wrong to use this isolated text to condemn the use of birth control.

Since the withdrawal method of birth control is the most natural, is it displeasing to God?

It is not wrong to use the withdrawal method (coitus interruptus), but doctors tell us it is not effective. Most men think if their ejaculation occurs outside the vagina, their wife will not get pregnant. But that is not true. Preceding ejaculation, a man excretes a small amount of fluid that contains enough sperm to impregnate the average woman. For that reason the withdrawal method is not a recommended procedure. In addition, it is almost impossible for the wife to reach orgasm through coitus interruptus.

Please suggest Scriptures on birth control. I have a friend who is going to have her seventh child—her fifth baby in five years. Her husband does not believe in birth control (except rhythm).

There is no clear-cut scriptural reference advocating birth control, nor is there one condemning it. The attitudes of Christians are changing on this subject, and thus birth control is gaining much more acceptance. The Bible was written long before such methods were developed; consequently its silence cannot be used to prove either point—as long as the couple does not refuse to have any children. We are inclined to believe that if the husband in question were to bear the eighth child, there probably would not be a ninth.

As counselors we cannot help but comment on the abject selfishness of the above-mentioned husband. He obviously does not have loving regard for his wife's health, energy, interests, or person. There is certainly nothing wrong with a couple having seven or more children, even in our day, but it should be a *mutually* agreed upon decision.

The problem of sterilization for either man or woman—is this really trusting the Lord?

If you "trust the Lord," you will have children. That is His will, as attested by the way He has designed our bodies—for the propagation of the race. The question really is, When does one quit—two, four, six, or more? Such a question each individual must answer for himself. We don't hesitate to have an infected appendix or gall bladder removed—is that "trusting the Lord"? We use modern science and medicine frequently; why shouldn't couples do the same with their reproductive organs once they reach the size family they feel they can raise effectively to serve Him?

Is it any greater "sin" to have a vasectomy than to use gel contraceptives?

Probably not, since both accomplish the same thing. But a vasectomy in most cases is irreversible, so one must be absolutely certain he does not want additional children before submitting to such surgery. We do not recommend vasectomies for men under thirty-five or forty years old.

COMMUNICATION

How can I learn to talk better to my husband about these things?

Sex is the world's most exciting subject, yet most people find it embarrassing to discuss. That is particularly true of married partners unless they begin immediately—on their honeymoon or shortly thereafter. Usually the longer you wait, the harder it is. Assuming that this question was asked by someone married quite some time, we suggest taking the following steps:

1. Pray for God's leading and direction.
2. Set a good time for your partner when you are not rushed and will not be interrupted.
3. Assure him or her of your basic love, then kindly state your true feelings—that you think something is missing in your love life and you would like to talk about it.
4. The giant step in working things out is for both partners to admit to a problem. In all likelihood, if you find sex difficult to discuss, you probably find it difficult to communicate about many things.
5. Try to get your partner to read our book *The Act of Marriage* and to discuss it with you.
6. Anticipate a solution—don't present an overbleak picture; you *can* overcome this problem with God's help (Phil. 4:13).
7. If difficulties persist, make an appointment to consult your minister together.

How can I communicate what I like, as a wife, so that my husband understands?

Talk frankly to him. If you are unsatisfied, say so. Most women find it difficult to converse with their husbands about sex, which merely protracts their frustration.

My husband had only "street" sex information and retains that attitude toward sex. This bothers me. What can I do? When I ask about my husband's long time (four-to-six weeks) without sex, he merely says he's been too busy. Is this normal?

It is hoped this book will help him. Once every four to six weeks is certainly less than the average recorded in our survey. Sex organs need to be used regularly to function at their best. Talk to him frankly; if nothing happens, he should get a checkup from a doctor.

How do you make men understand that women's passions rise and fall according to the cares and problems of the day and that their tiredness and lack of passion are in no way a rejection of their husbands?

By telling them so—gently—seasoned with love. Make sure you don't use "tiredness" as a cop-out. Do you take a nap before your husband comes home? If you are too tired to make love a majority of the times he desires it, you *are* too tired. You may need a medical checkup, vitamins, exercise, more rest, or a curtailment of some of your activities.

To what extent should a couple talk about previous relationships (some perverted)?

Almost none. The Bible teaches us to "forget those things which are behind" (Phil. 3:13) and "think of those things that are pure" (Phil. 4:8). Force your mind to think only of the good things of life, particularly those things that relate to love with your partner.

COUNSELING

Are the new sex clinics right for Christians?

That is too broad and general a question for a precise response. A Christian should always keep in mind when seeking any kind of counseling that non-Christians, no matter how capably trained, reflect different value systems than we do. That is what the psalm of the happy man means by saying "Blessed is the man that walketh not in the counsel of the ungodly. . ." (Ps. 1:1). What becomes acceptable behavior to Masters and Johnson or Dr. David Reuben may prove contrary to the Scriptures. Therefore all counseling should be weighed in the light of the spiritual values of the counselor. This is not to say that his instruction for severe cases of frigidity or male impotence is not beneficial. The more you know about any problem, the better equipped you are to cope with it. Personally, we feel that a Christian couple would be better advised to obtain Dr. Wheat's set of cassettes and spend two or three weekend vacations practicing his suggestions than to get involved with some expensive form of therapy, particularly if it admittedly lacks moral values.

Sexual dysfunction clinics are in vogue now, and because the state of California has not provided legal requirements of any consequence for such services, they are springing up all over. (Other states will doubtless follow suit unless protective laws are advanced to safeguard the public.) It is hoped some clinics are staffed by competently trained personnel, but that is certainly not the case generally. We know of two former welfare recipients, maintaining a nightmarish sex life, who have started their own such clinic and are getting rich at it. Some of the advertising circulars we receive indicate that many services offer little more than a new method of sex mating for a fee. Some of these sensitivity-group-therapy sex-dysfunction sessions reportedly end up as orgies. Obviously anyone would be advised to avoid these, and you should investigate your state's standards for certifying such clinics and the qualifications of any counselor to whom you go.

Where can a Christian wife go for help when there is a sex problem in her marriage?

Your minister is the proper person with whom to start. Many pastors today are experienced counselors, and you can be certain that he will keep your confidence. If he is unable to help you, he will probably be able to suggest another counselor.

DATING

I believe that young people need specific Christian principles to guide their sex lives before marriage. Could you please give the most important of these and tell why they are important?

Sex education coupled with moral principles should be taught discreetly by churches, but that issue is not within the scope of this book. We regularly share the following principles with our young people:

1. Your body is the temple of the Holy Spirit; it should be kept holy for Him. "What? Know ye not that your body is the temple of the Holy Ghost . . . and ye are not your own? For ye are bought with a price: therefore glorify God in your body, and in your spirit, which are God's" (1 Cor. 6:19–20).

2. Keep your body for your life's partner. "Know ye not that your bodies are the members of Christ? Shall I then take the members of Christ, and make them the members of an harlot? God forbid. What? Know ye not that he which is joined to an harlot is one body? For two, saith he, shall be one flesh. But he that is joined unto the Lord is one spirit. Flee fornication. Every sin that a man doeth is without the body; but he that committeth fornication sinneth against his own body" (1 Cor. 6:15–18).

3. Date only Christians, for dating is the prelude to marriage. "Be ye not unequally yoked together with unbelievers: for what fellowship hath righteousness with unrighteousness? And what communion hath light with darkness?" (2 Cor. 6:14).

4. Always conduct yourself as if Christ were present. "Whether therefore ye eat, or drink, or whatsoever ye do, do all to the glory of God" (I Cor. 10:31).

EJACULATION

How can a man delay orgasm long enough for his wife to get aroused?

First, by delaying entrance until she is ready— well-lubricated and her labia minora (or vaginal lips) enlarged two to three times their normal size.

Then after inserting the penis, by remaining motionless for one to two minutes to gain control. During this time continue to stimulate your wife's clitoris gently with your finger; this should have her on the verge of climax before you start thrusting. Avoid *deep* penetration and try to keep the glans penis between one and three inches inside the vagina to produce maximum excitement for the wife.

FANTASY

Is it wrong to fantasize as long as you don't commit adultery? Although I feel guilty about it, I find that it stimulates me. Three psychiatrists have told me that it's perfectly normal and everybody does it.

Fantasizing about a woman other than your wife is a fancy title for old-fashioned lust, which Jesus Christ equated with adultery (Matt. 5:28). The Bible has much to say about keeping our thought lives pure (Phil. 4:8), "casting down imaginations . . . and bringing into captivity every thought to the obedience of Christ" (2 Cor. 10:5). The mind is the doorway to the emotions or heart. If you think evil or lustful thoughts, they will make you feel lustful—"For as [a man] thinketh in his heart, so is he" (Prov. 23:7). Fantasizing will often cause a man to "use" his partner rather than "love" her; it tends to overstimulate, producing a premature ejaculation, and it creates unreal expectations. Just because something is exciting doesn't make it right.

How can I learn to control my thought life?

There are six steps to gaining control of your mind.

1. Confess all evil thinking as sin—1 John 1:9.
2. Walk in the Spirit—Gal 5:16–25.
3. Ask God for victory over the habit—1 John 5:14–15.
4. Whenever possible, avoid all suggestive material—i.e., most movies, questionable TV programs, and pornography.
5. If you are married, think only of your wife or husband; if single, force your mind to think pure thoughts about all other people—Phil. 4:8.
6. Repeat the above steps when your mind digs up old lustful thought patterns.

It takes from thirty to sixty days to create new thought patterns, so don't expect success overnight and don't permit your mind an exception. Gradually you will find it easier to control your thoughts, but periodically both men and women will face increased temptation in this matter.

If sex starts in the mind, should a wife try to "turn on" by thinking or imagining sexually exciting things? Like what? Are such thoughts (if not including one's own husband) sinful?

Yes and no. Yes—it is perfectly all right for a wife to visualize herself being embraced and caressed by her husband. No—a wife should not picture herself in the arms of another man; that is lust, which is expressly forbidden by our Lord. "But I say unto you, That whosoever looketh on a woman to lust after her hath committed adultery with her already in his heart" (Matt. 5:28).

21

I love my husband and am not at all infatuated by any other man; but during sex relations I have to fantasize some illicit relations with another man (never anyone I know). I am ashamed to tell my husband this. Is this sinful for me? Is it because my husband doesn't excite me enough, or what?

You have developed a very bad mental habit. Transfer your thoughts to your husband. Visualize past lovemaking experiences with him, or better yet, make love in a softly lighted room, keep your eyes open, and concentrate on what you are doing.

How much sex or possible lust should be allowed to fill one's daily thinking?

None. Lust is like a disease—it will grow. Bring your mind into obedience to Christ (2 Cor. 10:5) and cast down *all* evil imaginations.

FOREPLAY

Why is my husband always in a hurry to make love? He doesn't seem to understand that I need a slow build-up before I become as passionate as he is.

In talking with wives, we find this a common problem. For reasons known only to God, women and men are as different in their love timing as in their physical apparatus. Unfortunately most men just don't realize this fact. If they did, there would be far more husbands whose wives considered them great lovers, because time in build-up is probably the main difference between a husband who is mediocre in bed and one who is a fantastic lover.

Most men don't seem to realize that a woman usually prefers a long, slow burn to the instant explosion. Because a man is an instant igniter, he often makes the terrible mistake of trying to adapt his wife to himself rather than to satisfy her needs. It is a wise husband who adjusts his style to his wife's emotional pattern by beginning early in the evening to show love and affectionate tenderness, then gradually building his wife to a strong desire for lovemaking. When properly prepared, a woman's entire body becomes sensitive to his touch, and he can develop great personal enjoyment by watching her respond to his tender caressing. The old adage, Haste makes waste, certainly applies to lovemaking.

Is a woman's clitoris always the spot she desires her husband to touch to arouse her sexual tensions?

Definitely not. A woman is not a machine whose dials, levers, and buttons always produce the same effect. She is moody and cyclic, so her husband must be sensitive to her needs. When she is particularly passionate, a man can manipulate her clitoris immediately, but that is the exception, not the rule. Ordinarily she has to be kissed, caressed, and fondled in various parts of her body before she is ready for him to *gently* stroke the clitoris. Many wives complain that when their husbands learn about the clitoris, they often joggle it crudely as if it were a switch that is supposed to start their desire motor. The husband may ignite his outboard motor that way, but it won't work with his wife. Gentle tenderness is the way to arouse a woman's desire.

FORNICATION
Is there a difference between adultery and fornication?

23

The Bible uses the terms *adultery* and *fornication* interchangeably in some places and separately in others. Some people try to distinguish between them, suggesting that adultery is infidelity on the part of married people and fornication involves intercourse between the unmarried or when one is unmarried. We can't see that it makes any difference. Both are forbidden and condemned in the Bible, which states that "they which [continually] do such things shall not inherit the kingdom of God" (Gal 5:19–21; cf. 1 Cor 6:9).

FREE LOVE

Why shouldn't healthy young people who have to wait several years to think about marriage practice free love as long as they are honest with each other? It is a natural way to reduce their sexual pressure.

This question is increasingly on the minds even of Christian young people today. And it is a commentary on the effectiveness of the humanistic philosophy being offered by most secular educators. We propose the following reasons for preserving sexual intercourse for marriage:

1. It will maintain your spiritual and physical health. All sexual intercourse outside marriage is condemned in the Bible; consequently you will never be a strong, growing Christian while practicing free love. Physically it is hazardous, for it leads to promiscuity if the relationship is broken. The U.S. Department of Health, Education, and Welfare has branded venereal disease the number one health hazard in the nation today for persons under twenty-four years of age. A high school principal said recently that one out of every five graduating

24

seniors has either had or carries venereal disease. Thus free love is a risky business.

2. Sex was never intended to be an impersonal bodily exercise like swimming or football. It is an intensely emotional experience; therefore, sex without love before marriage inhibits a person from pursuing sex as an expression of love after the wedding.

3. Free love usually results in the creation of unfair and unnecessary comparisons. A Don Juan may be "a great lover" but an inferior person, whereas an excellent man to marry and father your children may be somewhat lacking in bed. Some wives prefer their husbands in every other aspect of life, but because of previous experience are dissatisfied with their lovemaking.

4. Guilt often rushes in like a flood after a person reaches thirty years of age, particularly in a woman, destroying a lifetime of wholesome love experiences.

5. It often keeps a person from finding the right mate later on. Like begets like—you won't find dedicated Christians from whom to select a life's partner among the free-love crowd.

6. Free love isn't free. A twenty-one-year-old woman wrote "Dear Abby," urging her to warn young women that "free love isn't free." It seems that she had been promiscuous since the age of fourteen and now had to undergo an operation to keep V.D. from destroying her life. "It cost me the opportunity of ever becoming a mother." The day I read that story, I couldn't help but remember the twenty-two-year-old Vietnam veteran who admitted to practicing "free love" while in the service. He wept as he said, "V.D. has left me completely sterile." There is no way in the world that a few exciting experiences in one's youth can equal a

lifetime of love experiences with a married partner, not to mention the joys of being a parent.

7. Free love is wrong. God's standards are not flexible, nor does time erode them. Virtue, chastity, and modesty are still the primary building blocks of marriage. Never has a woman come to me with a guilt complex because she has entered marriage virtuously, but many have requested counseling for the opposite reason. The devil has always been a "deceiver" of mankind; in fact, our Lord called him a "liar." Free love is a lie of the devil. Those who heed it are "not wise."

How should parents treat a son or daughter who is living with someone without marriage?

This is one of the most distressing experiences a parent can endure. As one mother exclaimed, "I would rather hear that she died!" We're not sure she *really* felt that way, but it seemed so at the time. Such an outburst, however, does display a parent's concern.

No matter what a child does, he is still your child and in need of your love. For that reason, don't shut him out of your life. He knows you don't approve of his conduct, and you may feel that you can't visit in his home without appearing to condone his actions. But we feel that you should welcome both parties into your home and avoid preaching at them or condemning them all the time—the Holy Spirit will do that. If you continue to express your love (but not your approval), when the illicit relationship finally blows up, you will be able to help them pick up the pieces of their lives. Read the story of the prodigal son's father in Luke 15.

Please discuss living together before marriage. My friends feel it is unfair to both partners if they cannot try it out for a while before making a lifetime commitment to see if they are compatible.

Such patently humanistic logic is expressly forbidden in the Bible. There is no guarantee that courtship or engagement will lead to marriage. Only a most unwise couple engages in premarital sex; in fact, it is the leading cause of guilt after marriage.

In our survey we asked the question, "If you were getting married all over again, what one thing would you change?" The number one answer was, "I would not engage in premarital sex." The survey also indicated that women who were virgins at the time of marriage registered a higher satisfaction level than did the promiscuous.

FREQUENCY

How often does an average couple make love?

Most researchers and writers in the field of sexual adjustment in marriage are reluctant to publish "an average" as a norm. Obviously people are not "average," but individuals. In addition, many complex factors must be considered: What are the ages of the couple? Are they raising small children in cramped quarters? Do they enjoy bedroom privacy? Does the husband have an emotionally pressurized administrative job, or does he do hard manual labor? Does the wife work, cook meals, and keep house? Did they come from loving homes? Are they happy? What are their views of married love? Are they Christians? What temperaments do they represent?

Dr. Wheat recalls a survey involving five

thousand couples, the results of which were fed into a computer; the average was two to three times a week. Dr. Herbert J. Miles's survey of young couples indicated once every 3.3 days, or about twice a week. A *Parade Magazine* article on the sex life of six thousand modern executives of all ages confronted with the pressures of business reported an average of once a week. Our survey taken from Christians who attended our seminars indicates that about three times a week over the entire period of marriage was "average."

Actually, whatever rate of frequency brings enjoyment and fulfillment to the two of you is "average" for you. A couple should not keep score on their love; they should be spontaneous, giving, sharing, and enjoying whenever it occurs.

How much does tiredness due to extended activities affect frequency of intercourse?

Tiredness affects frequency far more than people realize. Most people go to bed too late these days (after the eleven o'clock news); 11:30 P.M. to midnight may be great for sleeping, but it is bad timing for loving.

How can a wife have the same sexual desires as her husband?

It is not uncommon for a young wife to be aware of her husband's stronger sex drive and feel somewhat inadequate as a result. Caring for two or three preschool children can accentuate this problem due to boredom, tiredness, or both. But if she and her husband grow in love toward the Lord and each other, gradually improving their lovemaking techniques, the wife's desire for love will slowly increase through the years until she will desire him as frequently as he does her.

Does God expect a Christian wife to be compatible sexually with her husband? I feel unhappy for myself as well as my husband; I don't know what to do about it.

God intended the act of marriage to be a mutually enjoyable experience. Since the wife asked this question, she probably has not learned to achieve a satisfying orgasm regularly. If she and her husband will study this book carefully and experiment with each other accordingly, she will learn that art. Once that is achieved, her desire for the experience will increase.

According to Ephesians 5:22, wives should always submit (willingly and joyfully) to their husbands' advances. What if we are honestly tired? The times I have said no have left me feeling quite guilty, and I resent the guilt.

If you really were too tired, you shouldn't feel guilty. A loving husband can understand tiredness, even though he may be disappointed. But don't let it become a habit, and make sure it isn't an excuse. If it's just an excuse for resentment, selfishness, revenge, or something else, you will naturally feel guilty. "Speak the truth in love" (Eph. 4:15), then go to sleep with a clear conscience.

I feel I need sexual intercourse more frequently, but my wife doesn't want it. How can this be changed (we average about once every two weeks)?

First, you should analyze whether you "love" your wife or "use" her. Our survey indicates that many wives who have never experienced orgasm still enjoy lovemaking. They relish the closeness, tenderness, and endearment that always accompanies real lovemaking. But the man who is too selfish to learn the art of lovemaking and uses his wife to relieve his sexual tensions will never create desire in her for the relationship. Unless there are medical problems or deep-rooted emotional problems from their past, most married women's attitudes toward lovemaking reflect their husbands' treatment. It is a rare couple who needs sex counseling when the husband has consistently expressed genuine love for his wife, studied the art of coitus, and taken plenty of time for tenderness in foreplay and protracted cuddling after ejaculation. Consider these comments from women's responses in our sex survey:

—"Besides sexual foreplay, I feel a strong need of being cuddled and held after the orgasmic ejaculation, a soothing 'afterglow.' I feel that female orgasm in every intercourse has been over-emphasized."

—"Please stress how important a husband's treatment of his wife is during the day and how it affects her sex life at the end of the day (manners, temper, etc.)."

—"Encourage the husband to tell his wife he loves her, etc., during intercourse and at other times. Even though I know he does, it's just nice to hear it often."

We are so busy in our church (meetings in evenings, etc.) that it is hard to find time to fit in a love life. How should Christian couples handle this?

When married people are too busy for love, they are too busy! Nothing should crowd that necessary part of life into disuse—even the church. God established both institutions—the church and the home. They should never be competitive; instead, He planned them to be cooperative. When the church takes excessive time at the expense of the home, your priorities are out of balance. We suggest that you evaluate your schedule, and if you're really neglecting your home and family to attend meetings night after night, it is time to cut out some activities and stay home.

As a person looks to Christ more totally, doesn't the emphasis on sex become diminished and less important as true love binds the couple?

Looking to Christ doesn't change bodily needs and functions. Since Spirit-filled Christians get hungry, thirsty, and tired, why shouldn't they maintain a desire for lovemaking? After all, it is a perfectly sacred experience between married partners. Our survey shows that Spirit-filled Christians make love more frequently on the average than other couples in today's society. Besides, "true love" looks for an opportunity to express itself; lovemaking is the God-ordained arena for love's expression.

What does a wife do whose husband does not need sex more than once or twice a month (and the wife wants it two or three times a week)?

Have a good talk with him. He may be masturbating on the side, or he may just not be aware of your desire. Check your submission; if you are an unsubmissive wife, this may be his

31

subconscious way of getting back at you. Then try to be more seductive in the bedroom. Not many men can keep from being aroused by a sexually stimulating wife.

My wife enjoys intercourse when we have it, but how can I help her to desire it more than twice a month?

Although she may "enjoy intercourse," does she have orgasms? There is a great difference. The most exciting sensation any woman can experience is an orgasm. It is a rare woman who desires only two such exciting experiences a month. Be sure that your wife is having the real thing; you'll be amazed how her appetite for lovemaking will increase.

FRIGIDITY

Are some women born frigid?

With 3.8 billion people on the earth, over half of whom are women, no doubt *some* were born physically incapable of orgasm, but their number is so small that it is most unlikely any of them would ever read this book. Dr. David Reuben says, "There is no reason why every woman should not have regular and frequent orgasms, if she wants to."[1] To illustrate further that the problem is emotionally caused and not physically induced, he states, "No psychiatrist has ever seen a woman with this condition who was raised by loving parents in a warm, secure family environment. Most women who suffer from orgasmic impairment suffered serious emotional deprivation during childhood and after."[2]

One reason why we believe women raised in a

Christian home enjoy the pleasures of lovemaking more than others (a belief verified by our sex survey) is because they are more likely to have experienced a warm father-daughter love relationship. One of the best things a father can do for his girls is to let them run into his heart any time they like. He should avoid all selfish urges to shut them out or turn them off, no matter how busy he is. Frigidity is not usually a physical matter, but an emotional withdrawal from the opposite sex that can be well developed by the time a girl is six years old. Cold, selfish fathers are the greatest cause of cold, frigid women.

What can a man do with a frigid wife? I love her, but I'm not sure how long I can tolerate this.

It takes a lot of tender loving care from a husband and determination from a wife to overcome this problem, but it can be done. Please study chapters 8 and 9 in *The Act of Marriage*, and follow those suggestions carefully. A man displays considerable maturity when he understands that his wife's rejection of him is probably a carry-over from childhood and that he must *patiently* prove to her that he is not the same kind of man as her father. Every action should be kind and tender. Never raise your voice to her, but treat her with dignity and respect in public and private; gradually she will come around. In addition to this book, send for Dr. Wheat's cassette tapes, listen to them with your wife, and follow his suggestions. In short, love her as your own body (Eph 5:28).

Why does a frigid woman get married in the first place?

By no means did she deliberately set out to deceive you, for she probably never dreamed she was frigid. In the midst of unhappiness at home and at the time of her greatest sex drive (sixteen to twenty-two years), she met you and fell in love. Since lovemaking at best occupies only about 1/168th of a person's time throughout marriage, she probably was thinking more about life with you, homemaking, motherhood, and the other important aspects of married life than she was about coitus when she agreed to become your wife. Like swimming, skiing, or anything else, orgasm through lovemaking is an art that must be learned. The problem is, no other function in life so combines the emotional and the physical parts of two people like coitus, and this skill demands unusually concentrated practice.

I've heard your talk on sex, and frankly I wasn't impressed. Why is it that I don't like sex and don't want to?

You are probably filled with resentment, first toward your father and now transferred to your husband. Your shell of psychological self-protection has stifled your natural flow of emotions, making you a very selfish person. Unless you seriously begin to consider your responsibilities to God and the emotional needs of your husband and children, you will destroy your marriage. Emotional self-protection doesn't really keep you from being hurt, for it wounds everyone you love and consequently you yourself. Our Lord said, "Give, and it shall be given unto you" (Luke 6:38)—that is particularly true of love.

One of the most rewarding experiences of a marriage counselor is to observe women with this problem seeking God's help in giving sexual love to their husbands, only to find that they simply needed a little knowledge of anatomy and a few techniques of physical stimulation to learn the exciting art of orgasmic expression. It opens a whole new dimension to their lives.

GENITALIA

Is it possible for a couple to be so physically mismatched (too big or too small) that they cannot have good relations?

Many men are almost paranoid about the size of their genitalia, and women are almost as concerned with their breast size. Unfortunately ignorance usually produces ungrounded fear, and such fear proves a greater sexual deterrent than the size of their organs.

Actually, no matter how tall or short the man, his erect penis is almost always six to eight inches long, and as we previously pointed out, three inches would be adequate for propagation and wifely satisfaction. Similarly, no matter the size of the woman, her vagina will not vary more than about one inch. Research indicates that very tall men married to short women have the same ratio of sexual enjoyment as two people of the same height. Extreme difference in sizes may make it difficult to kiss during coitus, but there is no evidence to suggest that a man may be too large or too small for a woman. God's creative design has taken care of that.

Although I enjoy it when my husband stimulates my clitoris with his fingers, why does it make me feel guilty?

We are all influenced by our backgrounds, for good or ill. Somewhere in the past you developed the idea that pleasure must be sinful, like those who say, "Everything I enjoy is either sinful, illegal, or fattening." That's ridiculous! God has given us many wonderful things in life to enjoy, and married love is one of them. Nothing in the Bible condemns clitoral stimulation between married partners. Hebrews 13:4 makes allowance for it, and the Song of Solomon describes it (2:6). In fact, there is no other known purpose for the clitoris than to provide you with sexual stimulation. Your heavenly Father placed it there for your enjoyment.

To show how widely accepted this artful technique is in lovemaking, 92 percent of the Bible-believing ministers surveyed approved its use. (Keep in mind, only 17 percent of these same ministers approved self-stimulation.) We would suggest that you thank God for such a tender, thoughtful husband and enjoy the experience.

Ever since I had my hysterectomy I have been unable to experience an orgasm, and I have had an increasing problem with depression.

You reflect two problems—orgasmic malfunction and depression. Both are likely to stem from the same source—fear of inadequacy. Most women fear that a hysterectomy will render them less of a woman and incapable of sexual fulfillment, but nothing could be further from the truth. While it is true that a hysterectomy will eliminate your monthly period, there is no medical reason why it should interfere with your marital pleasure. In fact, many women have indicated a greater freedom and enjoyment in lovemaking after such surgery. But you must get over the idea that because your

36

reproductive equipment has been removed, you can no longer function normally.

The clitoris is the primary source of female stimulation, the lips around the vagina are second—a hysterectomy doesn't affect either. Besides, doctors have reported that in some of those extremely rare cases where a woman has had her clitoris removed, some were still able to experience orgasm. Remember that "a woman's most important sex organ is her brain." Unless your brain has been removed, you can function normally. But you must believe it. If you convince yourself that a hysterectomy is sexually fatal, it is; so face the truth—you and your husband have many good years of enjoyment ahead of you.

Depression is another matter. Most of the time it is the emotional result of the thoughts of self-pity at having to go through such surgery. Give thanks by faith (1 Thess. 5:18) and quit griping at God about it; you'll be amazed at how much better you will feel. If that doesn't improve conditions in a week or two, see your doctor—you may need some hormone shots. Admittedly this is an emotionally jarring experience, but self-pity only complicates it and retards the healing process.

Is it right for a Christian woman to have silicone injected into her breasts?

If you have already done it and your conscience bothers you, confess it and then forget about it. If you haven't, don't bother to have it done. A foreign body unnecessarily sealed into your flesh could present complications. Besides, you need to accept yourself as God made you—that's your problem. Except for exercises (and it is questionable whether this helps), there is very little that can be done naturally to change the size of your breasts. Many women who have undergone a mastectomy would prefer your problem to theirs. If the truth were known, the big-breasted woman may not be so sensitive to lovemaking as her envious smaller friend. The reason? Both women have the same number of nerve endings, but those in a large breast are more likely to be spread out further and not so close to the surface of the skin.

HOMOSEXUALITY

Is it a sign of perversion for a child to handle his sex organs?

Curiosity is the hallmark of every child, some more than others. Being curious about his genitalia and others' is natural to a child, and it is a wise parent who accepts it as such. It is best not to scold, punish, or shame him, for he is encountering an expected phase of growth. As he observes your relaxed attitude, he will soon get over his apparent obsession with the subject. You can use such occasions as an opportunity to talk over any questions he may have on sex. Be sure to use, casually, accurate medical terms for the various parts of the body so he will accept sexuality as a natural part of life.

It is best for parents to study up on the subject of sexual development and plan in advance how they will answer such questions. If you let your children take you by surprise, you will be more inclined to do and say the wrong things. A good book for parents to study on this subject is entitled *Sex Is a Parent Affair* by Letha Scanzoni (Glendale, Calif.: Regal Books, 1973).

What should be the Christian's attitude toward homosexuality?

This problem is increasingly rampant in the world today. In California alone, one prominent gay society claims to have 100,000 members. Some ministers are homosexuals and have started churches for them. My associate minister and I debated two homosexual ministers on a radio program in which they sought to justify their position. It was interesting to note that they could find no Scripture to support it. The only one they tried to use was Paul's statement, "I am made all things to all men, that I might by all means save some" (1 Cor. 9:22), a complete distortion of the apostle's meaning.

The Bible is very clear on homosexuality. It is an abnormal, deviant practice according to Romans 1:27. The children of Israel were commanded by God to stone to death homosexuals (Lev. 20:13), a severe treatment intended to keep them from becoming contagious. Every homosexual is potentially an evangelist of homosexuality, capable of perverting many young people to his sinful way of life.

The widespread propaganda emanating from secular colleges is moving society toward the acceptance of homosexuals as normal by removing all legal restraints against them. The governor of California recently signed such a law, overturning centuries of opposition to homosexuality. This will allow their number to multiply tragically. Though Christians are commanded to "love thy neighbor," we should actively use whatever legal steps are available in our communities to encourage lawmakers to enact laws against this trend. Christians are far too passive when it comes to using what freedoms they have to legally preserve morality and decency. Homosexuality seems to be the ultimate sin in the Bible that causes God to give men up, as He did in Romans 1:27, and to destroy them from the earth, as He did in the days of Sodom and Gomorrah and during the Flood in the days of Noah. Even while condemning the sin of the homosexual, a Christian should bear compassion for him as an individual and whenever possible share the gospel of Christ with him. That is the only known power available today to extricate a person from this awful vice.

What causes homosexuality?

There is no simple answer to this question, but this condition comes about from a combination of factors. One of the most common factors is an abnormal hatred toward the opposite sex aroused by a domineering mother, who "ruled the home," and a milk-toast father. This subconscious hatred of a boy for his mother spills over and makes it difficult for him to be attracted to girls his age. In the case of a lesbian, it is often the rejection of her father that prepares her for this life of perversion. Rarely does a child who is raised in a wholesome atmosphere of love from his parents develop a predisposition toward deviant sexual practices.

Another cause of homosexuality or lesbianism is an abnormal, smothering love of a child by a parent. This stifles his God-given instinctual response to the opposite sex. When a mother is not given love by her husband, she will often selfishly fill that void in her heart through an abnormal love for her son. Even though she would never think of doing anything immoral, such smothering affection sets up guilt complexes in the lad that stifle his normal reactions toward the opposite sex. Subconsciously he regards such feelings as a betrayal of his love for his mother. The same thing occurs when a girl is subjected to that kind of smothering love from her father, who probably does not receive sufficient love from his wife. Dr. Howard Hendricks has made the point at many of our seminars that "children need love, but they should always realize that they are number two in the heart of their parents. If they grow up thinking they are number one, they will have a difficult time adjusting normally to the opposite sex."

Normal love responses in children are most easily fostered in a warm atmosphere of love between their parents. This is so psychically normal that they feel relaxed in their attitude toward the opposite sex. Although parents should not be indiscreet in front of their children, it is good for them to see their parents embrace and display genuine affection.

Remember also that in their early teen years, as they go from childhood to adolescence, children are commonly attracted to their own sex. Junior boys, for example, often "hate girls." And as they begin developing sexually, they may find an unexplainable attraction to another boy or man. That is why they should be well trained in their home and church in God's standards of sexuality that boy-girl impulses are right and normal and that boy-boy sexual impulses should be rejected. Such teachings guard him through this ambivalent phase of life when even he doesn't know sometimes if he is "fish or fowl," after which he develops a healthy appreciation for the opposite sex.

When we came to California twenty years ago, we were ill-prepared for the many homosexuals I was called upon to counsel. But every case has followed a similar pattern. A boy with a tremendous love need met an evangelist of homosexuality who supplied that love need, at first platonically by "going fishing with him," "weight lifting," or just spending time with him. Little did the young person realize that he was being wooed as carefully as a man courts a woman. Then, when he was emotionally hooked and the homosexual act was suggested, the first thoughts of repugnance were swept aside by fear of losing "the only person who ever loved me." Little did the lad realize he was trading a normal love relationship of a wife and probability of children in the future for the satisfaction of that immediate love need.

You may ask, "Why, if they didn't really want to do it in the first place, do they end up confirmed homosexuals?" Because homosexuality is a learned behavior. You can develop an appetite for anything if you do it often enough. Once that happens, the person cultivates all kinds of mental excuses to justify it. Eventually his God-given conscience is "seared as with a hot iron," and he may become blatantly defiant in his sin; consequently another evangelist of homosexuality walks the streets.

Can a homosexual or lesbian ever be cured?

The answer to this question lies in the individual's being willing to accept Jesus Christ as personal Lord and Savior. If he is willing, a cure is possible, but so far there has been little success in any other treatment. As a prominent Los Angeles psychiatrist admitted, "Very honestly, I have never been able to cure a homosexual, and I don't know anyone else who has either." Unfortunately far too many psychiatrists, educators, and counselors don't even attempt a cure; instead they encourage the individual to accept it as not being deviant, "but another form of sexual expression."

One Bible verse is extremely encouraging to homosexuals or anyone else caught in a sinful habit: "With men it is impossible, but not with God: for with God all things are possible" (Mark 10:27). We have seen several turn to Christ and by His power extricate themselves from their dilemma. It is never easy, but with God's help it is possible. The following formula we have used with several individuals:

1. Accept Christ as Lord and Savior of your life.
2. Face homosexuality or lesbianism as a sin (Rom. 1:26, 27–32).
3. Confess it as a sin (1 John 1:9).
4. Ask God to break the habit pattern (1 John 5:14–15).
5. Walk in the Spirit through daily reading of the Word of God, and submit to its teachings (Gal. 5:16–25; Eph. 5:17–21; Col. 3:15–17).
6. Avoid contact with all former homosexual friends.
7. Avoid places where such people gather.
8. Cultivate wholesome thought patterns; never permit your mind to visualize deviant or immoral behavior (Phil. 4:8).
9. Find a strong Christian friend who has never had this problem, one with whom you can share your need and to whom you can turn for help when the temptation becomes strong.

One man I counseled years ago sincerely wanted to rid himself of this awful sin. He promised me he would never again go to the city park, which he had previously frequented to meet other men. As a further means of motivation he agreed that in his best interest I could ask privately, but at any time, "Have you been near the park lately?" Later he confided, "It was a real help when I was tempted to know that every now and then you would look me in the eye and ask that question." It is possible to break the habit without such a friend, but it is much easier if you have one.

Gradually the urges and temptation will diminish, but each time you do it or think about it, the habit is cultivated and becomes more difficult to overcome. Remember the sowing-reaping principle, you reap what you sow—yet it takes time. For example, your present feelings are largely the result of your thoughts and actions of the past thirty to sixty days. If you want to reap a better crop of feelings, urges, and appetites thirty to sixty days from now, then with God's help start sowing better seeds in your mind immediately.

Will children raised by only one parent grow up with a natural attitude toward their own sex and the opposite sex?

This question is near to my heart, because I was raised by a widowed mother. I was almost ten, my sister was five, and my brother was seven weeks old when my father died. All of us developed normal relationships with the opposite sex, and we can point to three happy marriages and thirteen children among us. In fact, my brother, who never knew a father, has five children and is a first sergeant in the U.S. Air Force with 397 men under his command. Obviously he relates well to men and women.

The Bible promises that God is "a father of the fatherless" (Ps. 68:5), and we certainly found that to be true. Actually it seems that a child without one parent can make the proper adjustment to life more easily than a child raised in a home filled with parental hostility and conflict. If a widow or divorcee has to raise her children alone, there seems to be a natural acceptance of her leadership role, and unless she goes overboard and smothers them, they will develop perfectly normal relationships with the opposite sex. It also helps if a mother in such circumstances simply assumes that God will provide the emotional well-being her children need. Then they are infected with the expectation of being perfectly normal, and consequently they will be.

In addition, it is always best to talk to children positively about their future. For example, never use "if" when looking ahead. "When you get married" or "when you go to college" is always a better term than "if you ever get married" or "if you ever go to college." A Christian mother's positive attitude, anticipating success in every phase of her fatherless child's life, is the strongest foundation for a young person, next to his heavenly Father's promise to be "a father of the fatherless."

IMPOTENCE*

Is it true that male impotence is on the increase, and if so, why?

Although no survey with which we are familiar compares male impotence today with what it was thirty to fifty years ago, most counselors will acknowledge that they face the problem much more frequently than they did twenty years ago. If,

*For additional information see the authors' book *What Everyone Should Know About Homosexuality,* published by Tyndale House.

as we believe, it is on the rise, the reason is more mental and emotional than physical. Most doctors suggest that it isn't a glandular problem, but is due to the emotional and mental pressures of our present society. Men get less physical exercise today than they did twenty years ago and have greater mental pressures to cope with. In addition, life in this present troubled world is less secure, and many men are less certain of their manhood than formerly. We look for this problem to increase as the women's lib philosophy creates more conflict in the home and continues to assault the male ego.

In the early years of marriage a man's sexual drive is about 75 percent physical and 25 percent mental, but as he matures, those ratios change until by the age of fifty it is 75 percent mental and 25 percent physical. That is why we say that if a man thinks he is potent, he is, and vice versa.

Do hormone shots help a middle-aged man's potency?

That depends on whether his problem is caused by a hormone deficiency. No amount of hormones will cure a man who thinks he is impotent. If the problem persists, a man should see his doctor, because a hormone deficiency can be ascertained only after thorough medical tests.

Does vitamin E really stimulate an impotent man's sex drive?

To date, published reports are inconclusive. We know doctors who consider it a waste of money; others recommend it. One doctor friend recommends 1,600 units a day for male impotence; another approves a Chinese root called *ginseng*. If you have a problem with impotence, it would be worth trying. If it helps, keep it up; if not, discontinue it. A one or two month's supply should give you an answer.

Does a vasectomy have anything to do with male potency?

Doctors assure us that the operation has absolutely nothing to do with a man's capability, provided that he doesn't use it as an excuse to consider himself impotent. We know five doctors personally who have submitted to the surgery; you can be sure they would never have done so if it would have affected their virility.

Please give some specific ways to arouse a wife when the husband is unable to have an erection. How do couples deal with inequality of sex (e.g., when wife is unable to respond, she can give; but when husband is unable to respond, he cannot)?

A thoughtful husband with this problem can lovingly stimulate his wife to orgasm manually to satisfy her needs. Usually he will find this stimulating, and it may result in the erection he needs. Most male inability is caused by the brain. If you think you can, you can. A wife can also help her husband obtain an erection by gently stroking his penis.

LOVE
Is it possible to enjoy sex without a close, affectionate relationship the rest of the time?

Yes, such a relationship is experienced by millions of couples the world over—but that is not

47

intercourse at its best. A couple who have learned the art of lovemaking will engage in coitus on occasions, but not so frequently or so enthusiastically as lovers. Love is an emotion that must be cultivated; no Christian should endure marriage without it. The first characteristic of the Spirit-filled life is love. If you don't have such love for your partner, you should examine your spiritual condition.

Is it really selfishness on my part to want to be more than a tool for my husband's sexual happiness? Is it wrong for me to want to enjoy it too?

Certainly not! Every wife has a right to expect to be loved to orgasm. Your husband, however, may feel extremely inadequate at not being able to satisfy you; and rather than admitting it, he covers up by acting as if it shouldn't matter. Talk to him, encourage him to read this book, listen to Dr. Wheat's cassettes, and consciously work on his lovemaking technique. We are convinced that any man can learn to become an exciting lover to his wife—if he is thoughtful enough to be concerned about her needs. Frequently all it takes is a little more clitoral stimulation before entrance and a little delay of his ejaculation.

MARRIAGE ADJUSTMENT

My husband and I were mismatched. Had we been Christians when we met, we would have known we should not have married in the first place. What can we do about such a situation now that we've become Christians?

First and foremost, slam the divorce door, which is not a live option for Christians. The Bible says, "Art thou bound unto a wife? seek not to be loosed" (1 Cor. 7:27). Now that does not mean that you must endure misery the rest of your life. God commands you to love each other; consequently you have that capability. Now that you have become Christians, you possess a new source of love to extend to each other. We have seen some rather impossible cases transformed into love matches by the power of the Holy Spirit. Learn to love each other. We suggest that you get a copy of our book, *How to Be Happy Though Married*, and put its principles into practice.

MASTURBATION

Is it wrong for a Christian to masturbate?

There is probably no more controversial question in the field of sex than this. A few years ago every Christian would have given an unqualified yes, but that was before the sexual revolution and before doctors declared that the practice is not harmful to health. No longer can a father honestly warn his son that it will cause "brain damage, weakness, baldness, blindness, epilepsy, or insanity." Some still refer to it as "self-abuse" and "sinful behavior"; others advocate it as a necessary relief to the single man and a help for the married man whose wife is pregnant or whose business forces him to be away from home for long periods of time.

To show the influence of humanism on people's decisions, we found it interesting that in our survey of Christian doctors, 72 percent approved masturbation and 28 percent felt it is wrong. By contrast, among pastors (whose graduate-school training was in seminary and undergraduate education often in a Christian college) only 13 percent approved self-manipulation and 83 percent considered it wrong. In most cases, ministers are not uninformed on the subject; they probably have to cope with it in the counseling room more than doctors. Certainly they deal with it among single men through their camp and youth programs. Among those who took our survey, 52 percent of the men and 84 percent of the women declared they had never or seldom practiced masturbation; 17 percent of men and 4 percent of women indicated they had practiced masturbation frequently or regularly. Many of these stated specifically they no longer did so since becoming Christians.

Unfortunately the Bible is silent on this subject; therefore it is dangerous to be dogmatic. Although we are sympathetic with those who would remove the time-honored taboos against the practice, we would like to suggest the following reasons why we do not feel it is an acceptable practice for Christians:

1. Fantasizing and lustful thinking are usually involved in masturbation, and the Bible clearly condemns such thoughts (Matt. 5:28).

2. Sexual expression was designed by God to be performed jointly by two people of the opposite sex, resulting in a necessary and healthy dependence on each other for the experience. Masturbation frustrates that designed dependence.

3. Guilt is a nearly universal aftermath of masturbation unless one has been brainwashed by the humanistic philosophy that does not believe in a God-given conscience or, in many cases, right and wrong. Such guilt interferes with spiritual growth and produces defeat in single young people partic-

ularly. To them it is usually a self-discipline hurdle they must scale in order to grow in Christ and walk in the Spirit.

4. It violates 1 Corinthians 7:9: "For it is better to marry than to burn." If a young man practices masturbation, it tends to nullify a necessary and important motivation for marriage. There are already enough social, educational, and financial demotivators on young men now; they don't need this one.

5. It creates a habit before marriage that can easily be resorted to afterward as a cop-out when a husband and wife have conflicts that make coitus difficult.

6. It defrauds a wife (1 Cor. 7:3–5). No married man should relieve his mounting, God-given desire for his wife except through coitus. She will feel unloved and insecure, and many little problems will unnecessarily be magnified by this artificial draining of his sex drive. This becomes increasingly true as a couple reach middle age.

As a divorcee, I have sexual needs that require fulfillment. Is it better to use a vibrator than become promiscuous?

Both alternatives are wrong and harmful. In addition, other alternatives should be considered. The use of special vibrators is not only acceptable, but advocated by humanists who regard man as another form of animal; many popular sex writers recommend them today. However, we feel they are dangerous and harmful to the psyche. The sex urge is basic in both men and women. It should be cultivated in marriage but de-emphasized by singles until marriage.

God put the sex drive in human beings to

inspire them to mate through marriage. If a single person satisfies that drive with a vibrator or other such means, his or her major motivation to marry is destroyed. It is also dangerous because it creates an erotic sensation that no human on earth can equal; if the person remarries, there will be a natural temptation to resort to this same practice because the human partner cannot match that sensation. This is "defrauding" the partner.

If it is wrong to masturbate, what can a widowed or divorced person do to control his sex drive?

We were confronted with this question by a lovely young woman whose husband had been killed in an auto accident. She asked, "What does a woman who is used to as many as ten orgasms a week do when she suddenly has no husband?" Admittedly she had a problem. She needed to know that (1) God's grace is sufficient for even her need (2 Cor. 12:9); (2) her stimulated desire would ease considerably in time with disuse; (3) she must guard her thought life carefully by Bible reading and prayer; (4) she must avoid all suggestive or compromising situations with the opposite sex; (5) she should become active in a local church and trust God to (a) supply another person with whom she can share her love need, or (b) give her the self-control to cope with her problem (1 Cor. 10:13); and (6) she could ask God to take away the craving (1 John 5:14–15).

Fortunately this young widow was a deeply spiritual person, and God supplied her need. Two years later she remarried, and she testifies today that God is able to supply *all* needs as He promised in Philippians 4:19.

A close friend of ours lost his wife of seventeen

years and confessed to a severe problem at first. He finally prayed earnestly that God would help him, and God removed that strong drive for six years. When he met another lady who finally became his wife, his normal appetite for lovemaking was quickly revived.

If my husband fails to bring me to orgasms, should I induce orgasm myself when he's asleep?

As a couple develops the kind of relationship that encourages open communication, the wife can make her needs known to her husband. A thoughtful husband who can't control his ejaculation long enough to bring his wife to orgasm can at least lovingly caress her clitoris until she shares his experience. The wife can help in this regard by faithful practice of the Kegel exercises. Many women develop such powerful muscle tone around the vagina that they can actually squeeze the shaft of the inserted penis enough times to bring on orgasm even before the husband starts deep thrusting. Those who have developed this art report that it introduces a dimension to the act of marriage they never previously dreamed possible. In fact, several women who had no difficulty reaching orgasm reported that even their sensations were improved by these exercises.

Is clitoral stimulation by squeezing the legs together prior to intercourse termed "masturbation"?

This technique is not well known, probably because not all women are able to do it, depending on the location of their clitoris, their body size, and other factors. We would suggest that if it is done to heighten sexual tension in anticipation of lovemaking, it could be labeled a form of foreplay. If practiced without a husband, it is masturbation.

MENOPAUSE

What is menopause, and what causes it?

Menopause, or "the change of life" as it is frequently called, is actually the gradual decrease of ovarian activity. Although there is great variability, irregular menstrual periods begin in the forties for most women, but complete cessation of the menses may not occur until they are well into their fifties. As a woman ages, her supply of estrogen, responsible for ovum production, begins to diminish; she will experience some changes in the lining of the uterus, producing irregularity. In some extreme cases, a woman in the menopausal period may notice a sagging of the breasts, a broadening of the hips, and an increasing weight problem. Some women complain of hot flashes, while others become depressed, weepy, and irritable. Any woman with these symptoms should see her doctor, as many of these symptoms may be controlled by taking estrogen. In most cases it can be administered in convenient pill form.

Why do some women have more problems during the menopause?

All women are different in temperament, mental attitudes, glandular functions, and body chemistry. The two biggest problems are—

1. A decrease in estrogen. Only a doctor can help this problem, but many women testify that medically prescribed estrogen transformed them during this period of life.

2. A proper mental attitude, which is more important than most people realize. The woman who expects menopause to "wipe her out" will usually not be disappointed; the busy, motivated woman who expects to take it in stride usually does.

Does menopause reduce a woman's sex drive?

That depends on the woman and her husband. Menopause certainly may create a problem within an already strained marital situation; in a few cases it may even overtax a healthy marriage. Some women find their inhibitions vanish as their menstruation diminishes. Current research indicates that many become more interested in sexual relations after forty than they were before. Much depends on whether or not the woman fears that discontinuance of periods will begin a loss in her femininity. Once she realizes that femininity is not dependent on having a monthly period, she can go on to many years of married love.

After menopause, intercourse may be painful for some women because the lower hormone levels cause the vaginal walls to become thin and less elastic, making it somewhat easier for them to become irritated by coitus. This can usually be avoided by taking sufficient estrogen or by using a vaginal cream locally that contains estrogen, which is absorbed there through the skin. Also, there may be a need for more artificial lubricant such as K-Y jelly.

It has been conclusively shown that women who have satisfying sexual intercourse once or twice a week all through the menopausal years have fewer symptoms of hot flashes, irritability, nervousness, and much less change in the vaginal walls even with little or no hormone replacement.

Can a woman get pregnant during the menopause?

Yes, it is possible. That is the source of the term "change-of-life baby." Many women erroneously conclude that because they skip a few periods, they can discontinue using birth-control measures. A woman can ovulate each month even without menstruating, and this is when she is vulnerable to pregnancy. Only a small percentage of women are likely to become pregnant during this stage, but there is no way of identifying them. Some doctors recommend that a woman continue using her birth-control measures at least one year after her last period. After that length of time, it is safe to assume that the ovaries will no longer function.

What can a husband do when his wife is going through the menopause?

On his wedding day he promised to love her "for better or for worse." Even if he may consider this to be the worst phase of his marriage, God expects him to love his wife anyway. Some women may feel insecure at this time and need to be reassured of their husband's love and their own feminine appeal. Her husband is the only one who can adequately give her what she needs: love, patience, kindness, longsuffering, and understanding. A husband should remember that God never requires what He will not supply; He will certainly provide him with the kind of love his wife needs if he is really interested in loving and helping her. She will respond warmly to such a husband and be appreciative when the menopausal stage is over. It is only a temporary period, and the years that follow can be long and full of tenderness for the understanding couple.

A husband can also help his wife at this time by seeking her companionship and including her in as many of his activities as possible. At this age the children usually no longer require her constant attention. With this lack of responsibility and extra time on her hands, she needs to feel wanted and needed by someone. A good church can be especially helpful to both husband and wife; fellowship with other people their own age and a place of Christian service can be rewarding.

MENSTRUATION

Is intercourse during menstruation medically approved?

Most modern medical authorities indicate that intercourse during the time a woman is menstruating is not harmful. It is untidy and should usually not be prolonged because the female organs are sometimes tender at that time and can easily become irritated. A woman may go from a warm, amorous mood to a chilly feeling suddenly. Interestingly enough, however, this is one of the times when her sexual interest may easily be aroused.

Does the Bible condemn intercourse during menstruation?

The ceremonial laws of the Old Testament required that a woman go through a period of "uncleanness" for seven days as a result of menstruation, and intercourse was forbidden (Lev. 15:19). Usually the ceremonial laws were for hygienic reasons as well as spiritual. But those laws were given thirty-five hundred years ago, before showers and baths were so convenient, before tampons, disinfectants, and other improved means of sanitation had been invented. The death of Christ, "once for all" has done away with the ceremonial laws, rituals, and ordinances (Heb. 9:1– 10:25); therefore we are no longer bound by them. We do not believe that intercourse during menstruation is sinful, but it should probably be avoided during the first three days of a wife's flow of blood and should be initiated only by the wife.

ORGASM

We experience simultaneous orgasms most of the time, but can't understand why we don't every time.

Nothing is more intricate than a human being. When the success of a bodily function is dependent on two very different human beings, it is unreal to expect 100 percent performance. When you consider that lovemaking is contingent upon two different brains, emotional systems, spiritual conditions, mood swings, fatigue levels, physical conditions, and reproductive mechanisms, you will realize that utopia every time is impossible. In addition, there are different levels of satisfaction. Admittedly orgasm is without doubt the most exciting single experience in life, but even when it is not achieved, there is a degree of satisfaction in sharing yourself intimately with the person you love.

It has long been interesting to us that professional baseball players are considered outstanding if they maintain a batting average of .333. That signals success even though they fail to hit two out of three times. Truly, hitting and pitching suggest competition, whereas lovemaking features two people in cooperation; consequently you can expect a much higher "batting average" from lovers. In all probability, an excellent love life consists of a very exciting orgasm 60 to 70 percent of the time, mild orgasm 15 to 25 percent, enjoyable love without orgasm 10 to 15 percent, and occasional malfunctions. Although you shouldn't allow the pressures of the office, nursery, or parenthood to invade your bedroom, sometimes they do, even with the best of sweethearts. After all, you are human.

Who should a Christian consult regarding lack of orgasm during intercourse?

Begin with your gynecologist. If that doesn't work, see your pastor and then a Christian counselor. If none of these prove successful, seek out others in these same three fields. Some are better prepared to help in the area of sexual difficulties than others. Keep trying until you succeed.

Do some women consistently experience greater sexual satisfaction through direct stimulation than through intercourse alone?

This is frequently the case, because it is easier to direct the hand and fingers to exactly the right spot than it is the penis. In addition, the vagina may be sagging and weak in muscle tone from childbirth; consequently it does not respond to the penis as it should. This can be corrected through exercise, and stimulation during intercourse can be enhanced through practice. It is very common for a wife to experience her first orgasm through direct stimulation, then graduate to simultaneous orgasm with her husband. Some women take longer to graduate than others, and some never do. Practice makes perfect, so keep practicing.

Do most women feel it is necessary to reach an orgasm for a sexual experience to be satisfying?

Most women want to experience orgasm—it is the ultimate sexual enjoyment, so why shouldn't they? God gave them that capability, and we think they should learn to experience it. However, millions of women never have the experience, yet indicate they enjoy lovemaking. We were amazed to note how many women who had never enjoyed orgasm reported that on a scale of 0–100 they would rate their sex lives 75–85.

Is there something wrong with a woman who seldom reaches an orgasm and yet is satisfied with sex?

No! It is hoped she is as easily satisfied in other things also. Then again, perhaps she doesn't know what she's missing. If she would have one exciting, exploding orgasm, we suspect she would no longer be so fully "satisfied with sex" without it.

Do most women really enjoy sex or submit to it only because they know they should because the Scriptures teach submission? Why do women enjoy it?

This question could not possibly be asked by a wife who experiences fulfilling orgasm. The woman who enjoys lovemaking and finds it her most exciting single experience usually desires it on an average of two to three times a week.

ORGASMIC FAILURE

How does one deal with disappointment over failure to find pleasure or orgasm in sex after seventeen years?

By making orgasmic fulfillment a prayerful quest. Study chapters 8 and 9 on "The Unfulfilled Woman" and "The Key to Feminine Response," in our book *The Act of Marriage* and carefully exercise your P.C. muscle as described by Dr. Kegel. Remember that 85 percent of the nonorgasmic wives so counseled have learned how to achieve orgasm this way. We believe no married woman should accept orgasmic failure.

If four out of ten women are nonorgasmic, how do they cope with this problem (to avoid the feeling of marriage failure and guilt)?

Don't cope with it. Follow the suggestions given above to a whole new dimension of lovemaking enjoyment.

How important is it that women experience orgasm during intercourse?

It depends on whether or not you are accustomed to settling for "good" or "best." If you can experience orgasm through your husband's manual stimulation, you can learn to climax your lovemaking with simultaneous orgasms—which is the ultimate, but an art that takes practice. Perhaps your husband inserts his penis too soon, or possibly he discontinues manual stimulation after entrance. You're almost there—keep working on it.

How does a wife reach orgasm with the penis in the vagina?

By waiting until she is sufficiently aroused before the husband inserts his penis. The telltale sign for the husband is not secretion of sufficient lubrication, but the enlargement of the inner lips of his wife's vagina. It is also important that he continue the manual stimulation of her clitoris for a few moments after entrance and that he learn to retard his ejaculation. He will likewise expedite the process if he avoids deep thrusting, but concentrates on keeping the enlarged head of his penis nearer the entrance to her vagina. Deep thrusting, which men tend to do instinctively, places the largest part of the penis in the least responsive part of the wife's vagina. Keep in mind that most of her nerve endings are within the first two inches of her vagina.

PETTING

What is petting?

Someone has suggested that "necking" is what goes on above the neck between two unmarried people of the opposite sex, and "petting" is what occurs below the neck. Actually petting is just a sophisticated term describing illicit foreplay by the unmarried, and it is dangerous. Almost all consenting girls who become pregnant out of wedlock engage in heavy petting before they are swept into intercourse. Petting is intended to stimulate passions in preparation for intercourse; consequently it should be practiced only by married partners. The price of petting should always be a marriage license. Most single girls do not realize that the time of the month when they are most amorous coincides with the time when they are most fertile and least able to control their passions; consequently it is the most dangerous for them when it is the most appealing.

Because petting is really "foreplay," it must be reserved for marriage. Among married couples it is usually considered their most exciting pastime.

Is heavy petting before marriage damaging to the initiation of a good sexual adjustment in early marriage? (It was to ours because of guilt.)

Most counselors will agree that your experience is common.

POSITIONS

Should married couples always have intercourse in bed? What other places are acceptable?

The bed is the most convenient place to make love for most people, but it certainly isn't the only place. Statistics indicate that at least 90 percent of married love occurs in bed, but almost all couples experiment with other places and positions when the mood suggests something new. It is wise to be creative and experimental at times. Any place that is mutually agreeable and does not betray your privacy is acceptable.

PRIVACY

How can a couple with young children at home really have the privacy to do anything they want in their sex life?

Put a lock on the bedroom door. Children should be taught to respect their parents' privacy; it's a necessary part of their training in recognizing the need to honor the rights of others. Besides, their parents will be better parents if they can freely and frequently express married love without distractions or inhibitions.

What do you do about lack of privacy with a teenager in the house? When do you relax and make love when you are afraid of being heard?

All couples should have a lock on their bedroom door, and children should be taught to stay out of their parents' bedroom. Locate children's bedrooms so that they cannot hear every noise that comes from the parents' room. Finally, relax—children are usually sound sleepers.

Should Christian parents expose their bodies to their children (as in bathing or dressing)? Doesn't supermodesty help to breed sex consciousness?

One of the harmful fads of humanism during the past thirty years is the encouragement of parents to let their children see them naked. This is expressly forbidden in the Scriptures and is unnecessary for child development.

"Supermodesty" is almost a thing of the past; we could do with more modesty today. Children should not be taught to fear seeing their parents naked but, out of respect for them, to avoid doing so.

ROMANCE

Most sex manuals advise couples to get away occasionally for an overnight honeymoon, but how can a pastor on a very tight budget afford such a luxury?

The first thing he should do is prayerfully examine whether his salary is too small in relation to the total church budget. If it is, and the church could afford to give him a raise, he should prayerfully consider having a talk with the budget committee when the annual budget is being prepared, forthrightly advise them that he is finding it difficult to live on his salary, and request a substantial raise. At issue is Matthew 6:33; if your first objective is to seek the kingdom of God, there is nothing wrong with your third or fourth objective being a decent salary to live on. You owe that to your family.

Asking your church for a raise, however, doesn't guarantee that you will receive it (though at least they will know how you honestly feel). Consequently you had better be equipped with 'plan B.' For that we suggest that you make your desire a special matter of prayer, for God will provide some extra work or a thoughtful gift from some member or in some other way make it possible. "Ask, and it shall be given you" (Matt. 7:7). It boils down to moving that "overnight honeymoon" higher up on your priority list—you and your wife need it!

We will never forget the thoughtful couple who rented a motel room in Palm Springs for us for one week back in the days when we didn't have two nickels to rub together. We can only wish that more church members would provide so bountifully for their minister and his wife.

You might also save the honorariums received from weddings and use them to improve your marriage by getting away for occasional "overnight honeymoons." Moreover, it isn't only ministers who need to get away from the children and household chores once in a while; every marriage will profit from such therapy. Even if you have to skimp and save, it is worth the investment.

SEPTEMBER SEX

At what age do couples stop making love?

While writing this book, we had lunch with two very close friends of many years. He is seventy-six, she is three or four years younger. We have long treasured their friendship and the sight of the beautiful relationship they share. When informed of our subject, he jokingly said, "I could tell you a lot to put in that book." Somehow I got the courage to ask him how often he and his wife make love at their age. He smilingly replied, "At least three times a week!" Then he added, "Now that I'm retired we have more time for that sort of thing." Obviously he didn't know that he was supposed to slow down, so he didn't! And that's the way it should be. Two healthy people should be able to make love into their eighties. We know several who claim that they celebrated their golden wedding anniversary by making love.

As a person grows older, the various parts of his body begin to wear out. But the process is as unpredictable as the people involved. Consequently some experience one malfunction, some another. When vital energies begin to run down in our maturity, many activities of our youth are pursued less energetically and frequently. It is not uncommon for senior citizens, particularly men, to experience occasional malfunctions in lovemaking. Unfortunately they jump to the conclusion that "it's all over" after a few nonorgasmic experiences. If they were to analyze their situation more carefully, they would notice something that gives hope and inspiration to try again.

Contrary to masculine obsession, a man does not have to ejaculate to enjoy coitus. Upon arousal, he can have a substantial erection, enter his wife, experience many minutes of exciting stimulation, bring her to orgasm, and gradually lose his ejaculatory drive. Instead of the usual high peak, his feeling just seems to pass without the customary explosion. Although it is not as satisfying as the ejaculatory climax he so enjoys, it does satisfy both his sex drive and his wife's. If he learns to settle for this lessened experience, he will still occasionally ejaculate, and as his confidence returns, so will the frequency of his success. Many, however, erroneously short-circuit their long-range capabilities by *thinking* that it is all over when actual experience would dictate otherwise.

What would you suggest for older couples who have had very little sex education?

Basically the same things work for them that inexperienced couples must learn, except that they must unlearn the faulty concepts and practices that may have hindered their love lives. Our counseling experience indicates that one is never too old to learn something new about lovemaking, and no couple should be closed to the possibility that perhaps something they are doing is not in the best interest of one of the partners. It is hoped the concepts in this book will encourage such couples to new lovemaking joys.

When one reaches middle age and feels too tired for intercourse, how can life be meaningful and exciting?

A person's sex drive parallels his other bodily drives. They decline together. Middle-aged people who are as tired as this person should see a doctor, examine their eating habits to see if they are destroying their vital energies with the wrong kinds of foods, or investigate potential vitamin deficiencies. We know of tired folks in their fifties who solved this problem by regularly going to bed one hour earlier. This gave them more zest. A number of people in our church have found that eating a large breakfast, a moderate lunch, and a skimpy dinner without an evening snack not only rids them of unwanted fat, but produces renewed energy. An increased sex drive will naturally follow and improve with an increase of vital energies.

Why does the desire for lovemaking fade as we get older?

Aging tends to reduce the intensity of most human drives, including sex, but by no means should they be destroyed entirely. For forty years I enjoyed 20-20 vision, but for the past few years I've had to learn to live with glasses. And that's only one of many normal adjustments we all must make as we grow more "mature." Because people live longer today than they once did, such symptoms are more noticeable, and because we don't get as much exercise as we should, we compound the problem. Most of all, a person's mental attitude is extremely important. If you think your sex drive is fading, it will fade. Most middle-aged couples are still enjoying all the coitus they want—they just don't want as much as they once did. Our research, however, has indicated that many such couples have learned to love better and enjoy enriched love lives through the years, even though sexual experiences have decreased in number.

SEX DRIVE

How do I cope with my husband's indifference to our sex life?

Have a frank talk with him—perhaps you are doing something that turns him off. Then try to ignite his interest by showing affection, displaying provocative attire in the bedroom or when no one else is around, and massaging his penis. Even the most reluctant penis can hardly ignore wifely stroking.

Is it wrong for a woman to have a stronger sex drive than a man?

No, your temperament, background, and general energy level will account for some of the difference. If you both approve your being the aggressor, enjoy it; never feel guilty about it. Many men are so mentally pressured by work and responsibilities that their sex drive is lessened until a loving wife stirs their attention.

What can a woman do to increase her sex drive?

She can change her mental attitude toward sex in general and work toward experiencing an orgasm. That usually increases a woman's appetite; repeated frustration often thwarts it.

SEX DURING PREGNANCY

I am pregnant (first child), and my husband is overly concerned about hurting me or our baby. This has greatly hampered our sex life. Is this normal?

You are fortunate to have such a thoughtful, considerate husband. However, his groundless fears are cheating you both out of many exciting opportunities to express your love for each other. Most doctors indicate that love relations are perfectly safe until about six weeks prior to the expected birth of your child. Urge your husband to have a talk with your doctor; he is the best one to correct his thinking on the subject.

STIMULATION

Should a wife stimulate herself prior to intercourse to get into the mood? (This seems wrong to me, but some sex clinics teach this.)

We see nothing wrong with this, but it would be better if your husband stimulated you through adequate foreplay. Self-stimulation is never as exciting as being stimulated by the person you love.

For a woman, so much of sex starts before the actual act. Women read books and seek help, but men usually don't. How do men get this education? What can a woman do to help her response when this area is lacking?

One of the reasons we are writing this book is to help such men. If your husband is not much of a reader, perhaps he will listen to Dr. Wheat's cassettes referred to on page 309.

Is it acceptable to use "playthings" for stimulation during lovemaking?

By "playthings" you probably mean vibrators to heighten stimulation. Those might be helpful in cases of male impotence or failure of a woman to respond to clitoral stimulation, but otherwise they should be unnecessary. In fact, to those who respond normally but use them as a lark, they might prove dangerous in overstimulating and establishing an appetite for a level of stimulation their partner could not provide naturally.

How many women get "turned on" by the sight of a man's body as men do from seeing women?

Not many. Women must cultivate the problem of visual lust, whereas men almost universally must cope with the problem just because they are men. Many wives indicate that at times they get excited by seeing their husbands undress, but that is more in response to the pleasure they anticipate than in what they see.

How can a phlegmatic wife be stimulated to an orgasm more often than rarely? My wife enjoys our sexual relations, but manipulation does not bring her to orgasm.

Perhaps you're not doing it right. If you don't get sufficient lubrication on your fingers, either artificially with K-Y jelly or the natural lubrication of her vagina, you may be irritating her instead of exciting her. Start out slowly and lovingly, then gradually increase your movement as her excitement intensifies. Discuss it with her frankly to learn what she enjoys best.

TELEVISION

I've heard of a medical doctor who advises young couples not to buy a TV set until after at least one year of marriage. Do you agree?

You are probably referring to my friend, Dr. Ed Wheat, who has proved so helpful in the preparation of this manuscript. He makes that observation

71

quite clearly in his sex education cassettes referred to earlier. Yes, we do agree with him, not only for newlyweds, but others also. Because of the busy pace and complex schedule most people are forced to keep these days, they have little enough time together. The hours they do spend in the privacy of their homes or apartments should be utilized in learning to communicate with each other on every level, not permitting the TV to absorb their prime time from after dinner until bedtime. Instead of talking, teasing, loving, and expressing themselves freely, they often spend the evening being entertained and consequently forfeit the much-needed sharing. This is particularly true in the first year of marriage. Dr. Wheat reports that many couples have gone out of their way after their first year together to thank him for that piece of advice. We noticed that our two married children seemed to have made exceptionally good adjustments early in their marriages; since neither of them could afford a TV while going to seminary and college, we concluded that a definite relationship existed.

TV is a thief of love, not just for newlyweds, but for most married couples. Wives with small children look forward to their husbands' coming home for an evening of fellowship, then become resentful when hubby can muster only a few grunts and nods between commercials. In addition, TV-watching tends to become a habit each evening until after the eleven o'clock news. Consequently, at least one of the partners is just too exhausted to make love enthusiastically. We suggest that shutting off the TV or at least cutting down on its use and developing the habit of going to bed regularly at or before 10 P.M. would increase the frequency of lovemaking for almost any couple. It would probably increase the quality of the experience also.

72

When measured in that light—TV just can't be that good!

TEMPERAMENT

Does one's predominant temperament also affect his attitudes and feelings about sexual relationships?

The more aggressive temperaments will usually be more aggressive about love; conversely the more passive will desire it less. Our survey indicated that Sanguines are very responsive to lovemaking. Choleric men are "quick" lovers and may not satisfy their wives; choleric women fall into two categories: (1) those who learn orgasm early will often initiate lovemaking; (2) those who do not will develop a distaste for it. Melancholics have a sensitive nature and can be good lovers, provided they don't develop the deplorable habit of letting their perfectionistic tendencies cause them to make a mental "checklist" of duties that must be fulfilled before they parcel out their lovemaking favors.

It was particularly interesting to us to find that phlegmatic women registered a higher frequency of satisfaction than phlegmatic men; but this is probably because a phlegmatic wife is more inclined to go along with her husband's desires.

Nevertheless, temperament is not the only factor that influences those responses. There are others—such as training, childhood, and proper sexual understanding. However, in our opinion, the most important factor that produces happiness in a couple's love life is not their temperaments but their ability to be unselfish toward each other. Selfishness is the enemy of love; unselfishness produces love.

MISCELLANEOUS

Do people shower or clean up after sex?

This is a subject we failed to include in our survey. Dr. Miles, however, did ask this question, with these results: 58.8 percent got up immediately and washed; 41.2 percent enjoyed an endearing conversation for a few minutes. Sometimes couples fall asleep in each other's arms. Usually the man can sleep all night without washing up, but because of the drainage of seminal fluid, the wife usually cannot.

When you refer to clitoral manipulation, do you mean other than with the penis?

Yes, with the finger. This is a necessary part of the art of love. Almost all wives can experience an orgasm with proper clitoral stimulation.

Why does a woman use sex as a weapon?

Because it is usually the last "weapon" she has—but why do lovers need "weapons"? When a woman uses sex as a weapon, she is grasping at straws, and unfortunately it leads to sexual suicide. Evidently she feels insecure in her husband's love. A man whose wife does this ought to respond in two ways: (1) talk to her lovingly and point out how it appears to him; (2) check his treatment of her—perhaps this dangerous practice is her frantic cry for help, and what she really needs is more love, tenderness, and consideration. Those attributes will automatically lead to a better relationship and more exciting lovemaking.

Is it ever wrong to resist a husband's advances? Is it harmful if done nicely with an explanation?

All spouses at some time have to resist the advances of a partner due to tiredness, preoccupation, mood, or other reasons. It should not be done often (1 Cor. 7:1–5) and should always be accompanied by a reason and an assurance of love so that the partner knows it is not a personal rejection, but a human limitation. This really should be no problem for two people who are so much in love that they are sensitive to each other's needs and desires.

My husband always wants me to be the initiator and him the responder. How can I encourage him to take the lead in the marriage act?

Have a frank talk with him and explain your needs for his expression of love. Your temperaments may be the cause—he is probably a phlegmatic and you are probably aggressive in most things. If so, accept it and do your best; look on it as a challenge to turn him on—you'll both be winners!

How can the sexual relationship be a spiritual experience also?

Everything a Christ-controlled Christian does is spiritual. That includes eating, elimination, spanking children, or emptying the trash. Why isolate sex in marriage as if it were in a category all by itself? Many spiritual Christians pray before going to bed, then in a matter of minutes engage each other in foreplay, stimulation, coitus, and finally orgasm. Why isn't that just as spiritual as anything else couples do? In fact, we believe the more truly spiritual they are, the more loving and affectionate they will be with each other and consequently the more frequently they will make love. Actually, coitus should be the ultimate expression of a rich spiritual experience that continues to enrich the couple's relationship.

Notes

[1]David Reuben, *Everything You Always Wanted to Know About Sex* (New York: David McKay Co., 1969), p. 141.
[2]Ibid., p. 127.

For more detailed information on sexual intercourse in marriage, see the authors' book, *The Act of Marriage*. If after reading this booklet and *The Act of Marriage* you still do not have your questions resolved, you are invited to correspond with us.

Dr. and Mrs. Tim LaHaye
Counseling By Mail
P.O. Box 16000
San Diego, CA 92116